Picnic

by Pam Matthews
illustrated by Olivia Cole

Core Decodable 21

Bothell, WA • Chicago, IL • Columbus, OH • New York, NY

MHEonline.com

Copyright © 2015 McGraw-Hill Education

All rights reserved. No part of this publication may be reproduced or distributed in any form or by any means, or stored in a database or retrieval system, without the prior written consent of McGraw-Hill Education, including, but not limited to, network storage or transmission, or broadcast for distance learning.

Send all inquiries to:
McGraw-Hill Education
8787 Orion Place
Columbus, OH 43240

ISBN: 978-0-02-143329-2
MHID: 0-02-143329-1

Printed in the United States of America.

2 3 4 5 6 7 8 9 DOC 20 19 18 17 16 15

Dad can pick snacks.

Nick can pack maps.

Kim sits in the back.

Dad and Nick stand.

Kim skips in the sand.

Kim has the picnic sack.
Kim has milk and snacks.

Dad, Nick, and Kim picnic.